M000311480

POLITICALLY
DIVIDED

A How-To Healing Workbook for Families, Friends and Couples

MITCH DEL MONICO

ROCK OTTER PRESS
LOS ANGELES

Copyright © 2019 by Mitch del Monico

Rock Otter Press
Los Angeles, CA
www.rockotterpress.com

Editor: Sabriga Turgon
Cover Design: Marilyn D'Amato

Published in the United States of America

All rights reserved. Scanning, uploading, distributing, or otherwise reproducing any portion of this book without prior permission is theft of the author's intellectual property, except for review purposes and except that which is in the public domain. If you'd like to use copyrighted material from this book, please contact permissions@rockotterpress.com. Thank you for supporting the author.

Every reasonable attempt has been made to identify owners of copyright. Errors or omissions will be corrected in subsequent editions. Any product names or companies identified throughout this book are used in editorial fashion only and for the benefit of such persons or companies with no intention or infringement of the trademark. No such use, or the use of any company or person's name, is intended to convey endorsement or other affiliation with this book unless specified.

The information in this book is distributed "as is" and is not intended to dispense medical, legal, financial, or other professional advice. Neither the author nor Rock Otter Press shall have any liability to any person or entity with respect to any risk, loss or damage caused or alleged to be caused by the instructions and use of this book or anything contained herein.

To report errors, please send a note to: oops@rockotterpress.com.

Quantity discounts are available for educational purposes, corporate gifts, fund-raising, or sales promotional use.
Please contact: bulk@rockotterpress.com. For other inquiries, contact: info@rockotterpress.com.

If you would like Mitch to speak at an event, contact: speaker@rockotterpress.com.

ISBN-13: 978-1-970128-01-7 (paperback)

Library of Congress Control Number: 2018965390
Politically Divided: A How-To Healing Workbook for Families, Friends and Couples
/ by del Monico, Mitch

Printed in the United States of America

For My Family

Without you, none of this would have been possible
or nearly as much fun. Our differences continue to
motivate and inspire me. I am forever grateful for
the love and laughter you so generously share.

Also, Mom, thank you for reading to me every
single night when I was a kid. Although it's far
from the only amazing thing you did, it made all
the difference in the world.

Dad, thank you for being the kind of man who has
a huge heart and values his family. Your enthusiasm
is contagious, and I love it.

And thank you, America, for being worth it.

Contents

Is This Book for You?

This book is for those of us with political wounds we'd like to heal. It's also for people who teach or counsel on the effects of political rifts. I'd be lying if I said it's a cure-all. I designed this book to help you get to know yourself, the issues, and your political opposite better, whether that person is a spouse, a family member, a close friend, or someone in your community. The important part isn't who the other person is or even who you are or have been. This book is for people more interested in who they can *become*.

This workbook also provides ways to steady yourself when dealing with emotions like anger, hurt, disgust, and disillusionment, though it isn't intended to take the place of mediation, counseling, or any of the other professional methods used for personal growth, anger management, crisis intervention, or healing.

It is merely a tool. By using this workbook, ideally you'll never look at an issue or someone with an opposing point of view the same way again.

That is my first hope, and my second is just as important: that you'll find reasons to laugh along the way.

Mitch

How to Use This Workbook

You don't need to read this book cover-to-cover for it to benefit you. Everyone has different tastes—and some of us just don't like being told what to do—so not every activity will work for you. Just remember that one of the goals is to increase your tolerance for certain kinds of discomfort, so make sure you're being honest with yourself about why you're choosing or not choosing to do certain activities.

If you're doing this with someone across the miles, consider using video chats for a more engaged interaction.

You also don't have to do this workbook in any particular order or even with anyone else. If you're more in need of self-care, you can use several of the activities just to help yourself understand why you believe what you do. Some activities are even meant to be done solo. If you're not sure which is which, look for the following at the beginning of each section:

solo

duo

☆ And for a visual aid to *Track Your Best Self*, photocopy p. 7 and use it after each activity.

Enjoy.

☆ Using this sheet to Track Your Best Self:

After finishing a chapter activity, use the space below to give yourself a score (0 to 10) for how well you handled it. Then rate the amount & quality of SLEEP you got / FOOD you ate / PHYSICAL ACTIVITY you did / MEDIA you consumed in the hours BEFORE doing the activity as either lousy 💥 or spectacular 🐧 or draw a line in between ⏱. How much did each of these factors help or hurt your ability to be awesome? This will give you a sense of when you're at your best so you can bring THAT self to difficult political conversations.

CHAPTER NUMBER | HOW I HANDLED IT (0 to 10)

_____ | _____

0   10
SLEEP RATING

HOURS OF SLEEP: _____

0   10
FOOD RATING

FOOD I ATE: _____

0   10
PHYSICAL RATING

MOVEMENT: _____

0   10
MEDIA RATING

TYPE OF MEDIA: _____

⏱ For a free PDF of this sheet, go to www.politicallydividedbook.com/tracker.

Introduction

If you're reading this now, it means I was able to overcome my fear that I wasn't the right person to write this book because I hadn't completely figured it out with my own *family* yet. It also means I successfully tricked myself into moving forward by saying that even if no one else read the book, I'd use it as a way to build a *relationship* with my family that included respect for our differences.

I'll admit right up front that I'm not great with conflict. I'm writing this book because after the 2016 presidential election, I didn't talk to my family for weeks. Maybe a month. It was a long time for someone used to talking with at least one family member every day.

When we did start talking again, we talked about everything but politics. In other words, we all ran from direct conflict. I spent more than a year avoiding political topics with certain friends and family.

You may know what this is like.

Still, it didn't make me feel like I'd found a solution, just a deeper hole in which to bury the problem. I felt like I only had two choices: pleasant conversations or screaming matches. I didn't see any other way to deal with the fact that we disagreed on issues that rattled us all.

For many, November 9, 2016 felt like vindication. For others, it felt like an earthquake. A lot of self-righteousness got hurled from one side to the next and back again.

It got messy and nasty and just plain ugly.

After watching the increasing divide, I knew there had to be a more honest and productive way to deal with our mutual dissent.

Before we go any farther, I want to address the proverbial elephant in the room: Could it be better *not* to talk about it, to keep the peace by saying, "OK, I see you over there. I'm not going to move. You're not going to move. Let's not talk about it and move on?"

It's tempting and fairly effective at maintaining the kind of familial relationships I thought I wanted. The problem? The result *wasn't* actually bringing me any closer to my family.

I had my ideas about what lurked behind our different views, but the truth was, I couldn't say for sure why my family voted the way they did. Possibly, a few of them weren't all that certain either. During the primaries I heard, "I lean more one way, but where is the party for people in the middle like me?"

I didn't have an answer, but I knew that if I wanted to have conversations about our sticking points, I'd need to ask myself some tough questions.

Believe me, I'd prefer it were easy. *Let's not talk about it* has gotten me through many conversations I actually enjoyed. Unfortunately, taking the easy way out doesn't square with my belief that I'm on this planet to become more human, not less. Our differences shouldn't be topics we avoid but topics we use to understand each other better.

We need to reinforce the idea that growth comes from conversations that allow you to have your point of view while recognizing it as an opinion and making the effort to hear what others have to say, too.

I also think we have to start these conversations at home and in our communities, learning to have them with people with whom the stakes are so high that we can't just throw up our hands and walk away.

Our country did not come together in the years that followed that era-defining election—if anything, the situation has gotten worse. At this point, every event slips too easily into an opportunity for us to destroy each other and our collective blood pressure stats.

America can be better than that. We can find a way forward that involves getting to know each other. Not everyone will join in, but maybe we can get enough of us talking that we can make progress. This starts with treating others as you would like to be treated yourself, although I feel like the Golden Rule should come with an amendment:

"Give others the same benefit of the doubt you give yourself."

This means re-thinking the belief that when I drive 5 mph, I'm looking for a parking space, but when the guy in front of me smacks the brake pedal like he's reacting to a reflex hammer, he's an idiot who couldn't find his butt with both hands in his back pockets. We need to get in the habit of coming up with at least three reasons someone might act a certain way. You can start by asking yourself three reasons why you might (fill in the blank). I'm not saying your first instinct isn't right at least some of the time. Just know it is not your job to point out all the blockheads in the world.

I care a great deal about our growth as a species and a nation and believe that change starts closer to home than most of us think. If we can learn to disagree with those we care about, we are so much closer to doing it as a country—because if the current trend continues without conversation, *We the People* will come to signify nothing more than the best failed experiment in representative democracy the world has seen.

The *activities* in this workbook can help you:

- *build* more authentic relationships;
- *learn* the reasons behind why you believe what you believe;
- *increase* your tolerance for hearing opposing points of view;
- *contribute* to the political conversation with an informed opinion;
- *expand* your problem-solving skills;
- *understand* the role of active citizenship in a representative democracy.

Don't worry if you aren't sure where to begin. That's what this book is for.

So let's get to it.

NOTES

Part One: Campaign Promises

Chapter 1 » Non-Disclosure Agreement

OBJECTIVE

Create a stopgap before revealing something you were told in confidence.

REMEMBER

The Golden Rule applies to information, too. Respect what's told to you by not telling it to others.

The purpose of a non-disclosure agreement (NDA) is to keep confidential the material about or information between the people who sign it. Think of this NDA as an agreement not to reveal something you were told or shown by the other person, even if that person hasn't specifically asked you to keep it private.

Even if you think revealing a particular story or bit of information won't hurt the other party, it isn't yours to tell. So don't. If you are unsure, ask.

To avoid any misunderstanding, this *Non-Disclosure Agreement* is not intended to be legal advice nor is it a legally binding document. Not even close.

What is it then? A solid reminder that you're trying to mend a relationship, not uproot it. It's remarkable how far that small step can take you.

ACTIVITY INSTRUCTIONS:

You may prefer just a verbal commitment for keeping conversations with the other person in confidence, but if you need a reminder, fill out the form.

If you don't like this Non-Disclosure Agreement, get together with the other person and write your own. Include phrases that make both of you feel comfortable and confident sharing your thoughts and feelings with each other.

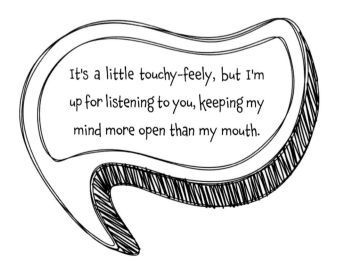

It's a little touchy-feely, but I'm up for listening to you, keeping my mind more open than my mouth.

N.D.A.

This Non-Disclosure Agreement ("Agreement") is entered into by and between _____ and _____ for the
name (You)   name (Other Person)

purpose of preventing the unauthorized disclosure of confidential information ("Confidential Information") as defined below.

1. Confidential Information includes any verbal, written, visual or other material that the Other Person has asked You not to disclose or that could be hurtful, harmful, and/or embarrassing.

2. Information Exclusions include any information that is publicly known or becomes publicly known through no fault of your own.

3. Time Period for this Agreement continues until the Other Person no longer considers the information confidential.

4. Binding Agreement. This is not a legally binding document. It's a trust-building document. What you're asked not to share, don't share. And you can expect that same confidentiality from the Other Person.

Signature _____   Signature _____

Printed Name _____   Printed Name _____

Date _____   Date _____

Chapter 2 » Rules of Engagement

OBJECTIVE

Create a list of effective listening techniques to help you learn what another person thinks or feels.

REMEMBER

Having an open mind means nothing if you only use it in service of what you already believe.

Conflict. It's one of the reasons you're holding this book right now. As with most interactions, understanding how to conduct oneself civilly can result in better outcomes for everyone.

It isn't complicated:

"Do unto others as you would have them do unto you."

It might not work if you're a masochist, but in general, asking yourself how you'd like to be treated if you were in the other person's shoes helps you avoid a whole world of hurt.

While our values represent our beliefs, they also reflect how we interact with others. All too often, we don't fully grasp the effect our words and actions have on those around us. Instead we assume others will feel exactly how we do, though that's rarely the case.

Fortunately there's an easy solution. If you wonder how you're impacting someone else, ask...then give your voice a rest and listen. One of the best gifts anyone can give us is the feeling that our needs and concerns are being heard. That's a two-way street. Yet when we're angry, we tend to forget we have ears.

For some reason, getting upset makes most of us think we need to say stuff, even though there's no evidence linking anger to our vocal cords. Much of it we'll later regret. Just know that "every time" is not the right time for a difficult conversation. You don't need to put it in your calendar—though that can help—but arguing behind the wheel of a four-thousand-pound moving vehicle is usually a bad idea.

ACTIVITY INSTRUCTIONS:

Can you believe moths have the best hearing?!

hold this up to a mirror

If you find yourself searching for the "right" word, you may want to try this word search. Locate and *circle* words that help you improve your listening techniques.

The next time an argument escalates and you're not sure how to respond, follow at least one of these suggestions and you'll be well on your way to improving your listening IQ. You may still feel angry, but you'll jump-start a pattern of respect that extends far beyond this activity.

A well-timed nod can be worth a thousand words.

Effective Listening Technique Word Search

Find and circle the **capitalized words or phrases** in any one of these four directions: ⇄ ↕

This is all about learning to LISTEN.

Use I STATEMENTS like "What I hear you saying is..." but not "What I think you should do is..."

Make EYE CONTACT. It's a different kind of "I" and it's just as important.

LEAN IN, keeping an open and relaxed posture.

Try NODDING affirmatively, not nodding off.

Ask clarifying QUESTIONS like "Do you mean...?" but not "Are you serious?" or "How can you believe that?"

Have NO AGENDA about where the conversation will go.

REFLECT the other person's feelings and do your best to display EMPATHY.

Keep an OPEN MIND and don't assume you know what the other person will say.

PAUSE before speaking.

Offer SUPPORT but DON'T SOLVE problems by imposing your will on the other person.

PARAPHRASE or SUMMARIZE what the other person says and VALIDATE the other person's experience, like "I'm hearing you say that crickets make lousy pets."

Know your hot-button issues and respond with RESPECT for the other person's shared humanity.

PRACTICE. You can't expect yourself not to make mistakes. Improve by learning from them and trying again.

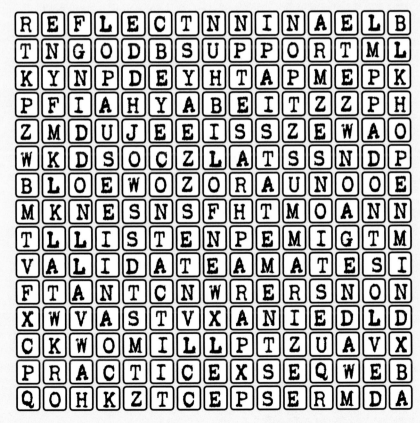

(answers can be found on p. 110)

Chapter 3 >> Family Values

OBJECTIVE

Create a visual representation of your personal standards so you can reflect on how your values impact your political views and how you treat others.

REMEMBER

You have your own set of values, as do others. Where you disagree isn't necessarily a place to argue but rather an opportunity to ask questions and know the other person more deeply.

Family values are often taught with the *intention* of using them outside the family, sometimes to the point that we forget to start by applying them at *home*.

We all learned a thing or ten about values growing up. Some of those lessons stuck with us, while others did not. Thankfully, most of us have an internal barometer about right and wrong.

However, even though many of us agree on basic values, we can't assume other people have the same definitions. They might, but getting to know others means dropping the assumptions we have about them and letting them fill in the blanks.

Consider this a chance to identify which values you care about enough to spend your civic and interpersonal energy on. It can also serve as a yardstick to help you monitor your own behavior, especially as it applies to those who hold different views from your own.

ACTIVITY INSTRUCTIONS:

Think about your most important values and write one or more on each leaf.

Next, translate those values into your personal *Rules I Live By*. For instance, if you listed *Compassion* as one of your values, its corresponding action rule would be *Open your heart to others, especially when it feels difficult*. If you're having a hard time turning your value into a rule, find a quote that uses your value word and see if that helps.

When you're done, compare your set of values with the other person's. It may surprise you to learn the values you hold in common, even though what they mean in your own lives may differ greatly. Particularly if you're doing this with a parent or one of your adult children, now is the time to reflect on the similarities between you.

Feel free to add to your tree once the other person shares with you, but only add your actual core values, not values you think you should have or someone else expects you to have.

Build Your Family Values Tree

write values on leaf veins

Rules to Live By

_____

_____

_____

NOTES

Part Two: Primaries

Chapter 4 » Learning to Walk a Mile

OBJECTIVE

Take small steps to see life from the other person's point of view.

REMEMBER

Life's value comes from the effort. Make mistakes; reaching your goal is a bonus.

They say that babies learning to walk take *thousands* of steps and have dozens of wipeouts *each day*. To accomplish that, they abandon a relatively stable position for one where falling is as common as thumb-sucking.

While those first steps deserve our applause, it's all the "steps" beforehand that make it possible: head lifting, belly surfing, sitting, crawling, scooting, standing, walking with assistance, and more—all of which help the child develop the balance, muscles, exploratory skills, and confidence necessary to walk.

action + mistakes + learning + time = growth
REPEAT.

Let's face it: human beings are imperfect. When we use this fact as an opportunity for investigation and growth, we let go of the fear that our mistakes define us.

Setting out to achieve our goals, we often make plans that overwhelm us, in part because we overestimate how much we can accomplish in a single day, week, or year at the same time as we underestimate the value of baby steps.

It's important to note that while parents—and researchers—often try to direct infants along a singular path, babies prefer to start, stop, speed up, slow down, miss a step, swerve in all directions, fall down, then get up and try again in a variety of situations. They seem to understand that different learning environments will require different strategies and they can't just replay their greatest hits. Nor do they do this continuously. Throughout the day, they include bouts of rest in which they consolidate their learning and renew motivation.

When it comes to our political differences, we have to start small if we hope to make any long-term progress. We need to take breaks, try things in a variety of situations, and recognize a mental rut when we see one.

Change is hard. I've been as guilty as the next person of thinking that I could change *something* without changing *anything*, without putting in the work over time to replace unhelpful habits with ones that get me closer to my goals. As humans, we have a lot of inconsistencies. We may hope that others don't notice them, but even if they don't, you are there to witness yourself. If it's an inconsistency you can live with, carry on. If not—and I'm saying this as much to myself as to you—do the work to change it. Your future self thanks you.

ACTIVITY INSTRUCTIONS:

Once we learn to walk, we can learn to walk in someone else's shoes. It's one of the first steps in repairing your politically divided relationships. To learn more about how the other person thinks, do this activity together. If you don't feel up to it, do it apart and then talk about your answers.

JUST YOUR AVERAGE AMERICAN

How would you describe the average American? Use the first image that pops into your mind, even if it doesn't necessarily fit with your beliefs or worldview.

_____

How do you think that image got associated with your idea about an average American?

_____

What 3 things do you think people from another country believe about Americans?

_____   _____   _____

What 3 things would you like people from another country to know about Americans?

_____   _____   _____

WHAT DIPLOMATS KNOW

Pick a country. It can be a random selection, but use the same one as the other person. What 3 things do you believe about citizens of that country? Think about how you formed those ideas.

_____   _____   _____

Write down anything you know about the political system of the country you selected above.

_____

Spend 5 minutes researching that country's government or people. Write down 3 things you learned.

_____   _____   _____

Select a hot-button issue, ideally one you disagree with the other person about. What does the debate on that issue look like in the country you selected above? What are the pros and cons? Do they have different considerations than ours?

_____

What is 1 thing you learned from looking at how another country approaches the issue and 1 thing you can do to contribute to solving the problem in our country?

_____   _____

Chapter 5 » They Don't Call 'em Strong Feelings for Nothing

OBJECTIVE

Find your comfort zone and learn how to navigate outside of it.

REMEMBER

When discussing contentious political issues, the other person is navigating uncomfortable feelings and learning new behaviors, too.

Everyone has a comfort zone, and talking productively about differing political issues requires you to step outside your own. Not only is it uncomfortable but trying something new brings a lot of what I call *fast-twitch feelings*: compelling, powerful feelings that fatigue faster and require more time for recovery—like rage, amazement, and terror. Slow-twitch feelings—like satisfaction or contempt—aren't as muscular but tend to be more *sustainable* over long periods of time.

And like with muscles, working on your feelings can lead to improvements, but when you repeat the same exercises without variation, you'll plateau. *Hitting a wall* not only means reaching a point at which you feel stuck. It means feeling stuck in ways that can make you forget the advances you've made in the past, with frustration and self-doubt following right behind.

One way to break through this sticking point is to give up. Wait, what?

Although giving up may sound like bad advice, I don't mean shrugging your shoulders and saying *oh well*—or something less G-rated. I'm talking about giving up old ways. To remind you of yet another overused wall metaphor: the only time hitting your head against a brick wall feels good is when you stop.

Most of us know from experience that the way to break through feeling stuck involves doing something different, creating variations or completely new habits to replace ones that no longer work or (let's be honest) never worked all that well in the first place. To do this requires stepping outside our comfort zones and looking at fear for what it often is: a reflection of our deepest insecurities. Because it's scary, a lot of us don't even try.

Doing something outside your comfort zone can bring up feelings of anxiety, uncertainty, and may even make you a little sick to your stomach. The good news? You can make this sort of discomfort familiar and valuable enough that you no longer avoid it at all costs.

This works for other sorts of discomfort, too—just ask anyone who's figured out how to stick to a workout routine.

A word of caution: Getting out of your comfort zone doesn't mean leaping without a look. Although taking a risk can feel scary, it doesn't have to involve physical danger. If something is uncomfortable because you feel unsafe, assess the actual threat before proceeding.

If you're having trouble evaluating it, ask someone you trust to help you figure it out. Consulting others helps you take controlled risks, which means you can rehearse, checking for potential obstacles and brainstorming solutions beforehand. It also means you have a goal, a plan, and a back-up plan in case your first idea doesn't work out. Just don't get so caught up in the planning that you forget the objective involves *doing* something outside your comfort zone, not just thinking about it.

ACTIVITY INSTRUCTIONS:

This activity will give you some ideas for getting out of your comfort zone, but you're the expert on what this means for you. Get creative, and consider involving the other person. Perhaps you'd both like to learn ten phrases in Finnish or Hindi or Xhosa. There's no rule that says this can't be fun. Even if you don't live near each other, you can find ways to collaborate or just check in about your progress.

Your COMFORT ZONE is not the best spot to find magic.

Also consider doing one *political activity* that feels outside your comfort zone. It could be as simple as reading a chapter or an article by an author whose views don't align with yours. I recommend doing this activity offline as much as possible—or at the very least, staying away from any online activity that includes trolling or a comments section.

Afterward, tell the other person what new political activity you tried. Don't go into specifics, just talk about the *feelings* you had during the experience. Don't just talk about anger either. It's likely that when someone expresses a political opinion that differs from yours, you not only feel mad, you feel uncomfortable. Now is the chance to investigate why. Maybe the opinion feels at odds with a value you hold or with one you believe the other person holds. This is a great chance to practice your new and improved active listening techniques, too.

I've included some ideas for getting out of your comfort zone in the pages that follow, but it's just to get you started. Find challenges that work for you.

23

Life Outside Your Comfort Zone

Looking for ways to get used to the feeling of trying something different?

Try a new restaurant with food prepared in a way you've never had before.

Listen to a singer or band whose name you don't recognize.

Read a book by an author you've never heard of.

Remember that person you said you'd follow up with? Schedule a time to meet up.

Wear a piece of clothing you've been waiting for the "right occasion" to wear.

Go to a public talk or lecture on a subject that interests you but you know little about.

TURN OFF
2-WAY RADIO
AND
CELL PHONE

Ride or walk to work in silence.

Get out of your own way and be bigger than you think you are. Be the lion inside.

Bottom line: Get out of your comfort zone!

NOTES

Part Three: Attack Ads

Chapter 6 » Improving Your @#$%&! Vocabulary

OBJECTIVE

Express anger safely and inspect the feelings that often get submerged beneath it.

REMEMBER

Remove this page if you think there's a chance the other person will see it. The benefit comes from being able to unfilter yourself without damaging relationships.

Let's face it, when we're angry, calling each other names feels great—in the moment. We usually realize later that not only do we need to apologize, we probably shouldn't have said it from the start.

When we call each other names, admittedly there's a bit of laziness involved. Calling someone a @#$%&! means you don't have to consider—and then describe—what actually bothers you. You know, the heart of the issue.

Don't get me wrong; a rapid bleep-worthy word has its uses, but most of the appropriate ones happen when you're alone.

What to do with all those pent-up verbal gems? Fear not: you can let 'em out here. Get your feelings about the other person's political beliefs out of your system. Make it personal but keep it factual.

Then shred it or cover it with black marker if there's a chance someone else will see it, especially the person it's about.

ACTIVITY INSTRUCTIONS:

Need a laugh? Want to improve your mood? If you've never seen one of these word games before, it uses the same principle as Mad Libs®, that word game in which one player prompts the other to fill in the blanks of a story without knowing anything other than which parts of speech to provide.

For the *person who answers* the parts of speech, you may find it more spontaneous if you don't look at the activity ahead of time, but unless you've got a photographic memory, it'll still work if you do.

For the *person who asks for* the parts of speech, instruct the other person to answer with the first thing that comes to mind. It's more fun if you keep politics out of it, so if you do this after a difficult political conversation or activity, maybe say the alphabet first as a palate cleanser.

And feel free to skip the following definitions if you've already aced parts of speech.

PARTS OF SPEECH:

NOUN: a word for a person, place, animal, thing, or idea (e.g., cat, building, democracy).

PROPER NOUN: a name used for a person, place, or organization; something you'd write with its first letter capitalized (e.g., Garfield, Empire State Building, U.S. Constitution).

ADJECTIVE: a word or phrase that describes or modifies a noun (e.g., orange, short, apolitical).

SUPERLATIVE ADJECTIVE: a word or phrase that compares three or more nouns to their highest degree; many superlative adjectives end in –est (e.g., funniest, nicest, best).

VERB: a word describing an action, occurrence, or a state of being or doing (e.g., shred, walk, underestimate).

GERUND: a verb that ends in –ing and acts like a noun (e.g., Reading can teach you a lot.).

ADVERB: a word or phrase that enhances, modifies, or qualifies an adjective, verb, or another adverb; many adverbs end in –ly (e.g., accidentally, bravely, empathetically).

TEMPORAL ADVERB: related to time, the temporal adverb answers the question *when*? (e.g., later, soon, tomorrow).

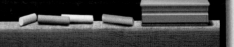

The Angry Ad Lib

Name-calling for the name-calling challenged.

Date: /   /

What in the world was _____ thinking when s/he voted for that
                        (first name)

_____ , knowing full well that _____ are so
      (noun)   (team mascot, plural)

_____ ?! It's obvious that my _____ was the
      (adjective)   (job title)

better candidate.

Since the election, I wake up every morning in a(n)_____ mood
                                                     (cartoon character)

and have a strong desire to drink _____ . Instead I wind up eating
                                     (noun, beverage)

_____ for breakfast and watching _____ _____
   (noun, plural)   (adjective)   (noun, plural)

chase each other up and down the telephone pole. This may seem _____
                                                                  (adjective)

but you have to see it from _____ 's point of view.
                              (famous historical figure)

Maybe_____ are what we all need, but for now I'm just going to call
       (noun, plural)

you a(n) _____ _____ . I'll get it out of my _____ .
          (adjective)   (noun)   (body part)

If you like, you can call me the _____ _____ you've
                                  (superlative adjective)   (animal)

ever known.

I can worry about this _____ manure _____ when I'll start
                          (noun)   (temporal adverb)

fresh by promising to eliminate all the lawn _____ from
                                               (wild animal, plural)

my life. I spend too much time _____ anyway. How about you?
                                  (gerund)

Chapter 7 » Your Brain on Anger (and What to Do About It)

The brain may only make up about 2% of our total body weight, but it has a disproportionate amount of clout in our daily lives. While a bit of the brain thankfully stays occupied with *essentials* like breathing, digestion, and more, it's the job of our frontal lobes to make sure we engage in those mental processes we like to call *thinking*. This includes making decisions and planning ahead. When we're at our best, this part of our brain fires on all cylinders, but when we're angry, our brain circuitry is working on fumes.

So why do we even get angry? From a survival standpoint, we get angry because we feel threatened physically or emotionally. In order to conserve energy, our frontal lobes go offline so our limbic system can work on making us safe. Great, right?

Not always. Too often, we see threats where there are none, but with our frontal lobes offline, it's nearly impossible to differentiate that. That's why people suggest taking a deep breath when you're mad. Breathing deeply through your nose sends a message to your brain that everything is OK, no need for stress. It also forces you to focus on something other than whatever upset you. Counting to ten does essentially the same thing: it slows you down enough to assess rather than react.

Although anger is a natural emotion, it's a very inefficient way to communicate with people you disagree with (or even with disagreeable people). The reason it's so tempting is because it puts us in a perceived safe zone: one of certainty. In essence, thinking *I'm right* and *you're wrong* is nothing more than your brain quieting the discomfort that comes from disagreeing with someone.

If you want to have a productive conversation, creating a situation in which the other person feels threatened just won't work. The more stressed people feel, the less they're able to process new information and remain open to what you're saying.

In other words, when you yell at someone, the only thing you accomplish is disabling the other person's ability to think rationally as well.

But what actually happens in your body when you're mad?

Anger is a physiological as well as an emotional process—your adrenal glands flood the body with stress hormones; your heart rate, blood pressure, and respiratory rate go up. Picture

OBJECTIVE

Become aware of the short-term and long-term effects of what happens in your brain when you're angry.

REMEMBER

Anger doesn't excuse hurtful behavior or words. You're still responsible for anything you say or do, even when you're upset.

31

the long game and ask yourself: Whom is your anger *really* hurting?

The next time you're upset, try giving your prefrontal cortex more of a fighting chance than your rage. I promise, your brain is up to the challenge.

Heck, the whole body is kind of incredible when you think about it. So think about it! Take a few minutes to write down three things you're grateful your body can do.

How could your unchecked anger negatively affect that?

1. _____

_____

2. _____

_____

3. _____

_____

ACTIVITY INSTRUCTIONS:

Because you're alive, you may think your body is already an expert at breathing, but many of us underuse our lungs and overuse our neck and chest muscles when we breathe.

After our daily bout of around 20,000 breaths, the impact of inefficient breathing adds up and can contribute to headaches, neck stiffness, back pain, and more. Obviously, this increases our irritability and puts us in a less open state of mind.

Fortunately, you don't need any special equipment to improve your breathing techniques, just the incredible body you were born with.

☘ Breathing <u>is</u> inspiring. ☘

Breathing Exercises

Inefficient breathing patterns become habits, so leave them in the dust and learn to breathe more effectively.

⚘ Pursed Lips Breathing ⚘

1. Relax your neck and shoulders.
2. With your mouth closed, breathe in through your nostrils for a count of two.
3. Pucker or purse your lips like you were giving a kiss.
4. Breathe out through your puckered lips for a count of four.
5. If able, repeat several times throughout the day.

⚘ Helpful Hints ⚘

There's no need to force the air in or out. You don't have to take a deep breath for pursed lip breathing to benefit you—although for it to be most effective, you should breathe out longer than you breathe in.

⚘ Diaphragmatic (Belly) Breathing ⚘

1. Lie on your back, either with knees bent or a pillow underneath your knees.
2. Place your hands lightly, one on your chest and one on your belly.
3. Breathe in through your nostrils slowly, feeling your belly push against your hand as air fills your lungs.
4. Breathe out slowly through your lips. You should feel your belly fall inward.
5. If able, repeat several times throughout the day.

⚘ Helpful Hints ⚘

Your diaphragm muscles will get stronger with consistent practice, but that doesn't mean your stomach will expand! It's just really hard to inhale (and contract your diaphragm) without your belly sticking out. It's also hard to exhale (and relax your diaphragm) without your belly falling inward. Breathing isn't meant to be hard, so relax and take the easy way out.

What takes YOUR breath away?

_____

Be awe-filled. Not awful.

Chapter 8 » Why Do I Hate You So Much Right Now?!

OBJECTIVE

Add more tools to your anger management toolbox.

REMEMBER

It isn't so much anger itself but how we handle it that can impact our well-being and our relationships. Your reaction is a choice; choose like your health depends on it, because it does!

We've all experienced feeling so mad at someone that we think we hate them—multiply by a thousand if you or the other person is going through puberty. However, it's important to *remember* that even in those *moments*, you probably don't.

Believe it or not, there are stages to anger. It may feel like a rocket launch without the countdown, but now that you've improved your breathing techniques, those ten seconds—before your own explosive liftoff—may be all you need to craft a more civil response.

But what if the breathing techniques just aren't getting the job done? What if you find yourself in a heated argument with the other person, and the only thing deep breathing has accomplished is more oxygen for yelling? In addition to the chapter activity, try asking yourself: *How much do I love this person right now?*

It's not the first thing most of us would think in that situation, but you can get there. Maybe substitute: *On any other day, how much do I love this person?* The difference between those answers is what you're working to reduce.

Not only is our time on this planet finite, the other person's is, too. So if the other questions don't work for you, try: *What would I lose if I lost this person, if I could never talk to this person again, for whatever reason?* Because here's the truth: you can't get that time back—the empty chair around the table, the missed conversations, the smiles, laughter, and vibrant moments with the person you're angry at. I repeat: You can't get that time back. Act accordingly.

ACTIVITY INSTRUCTIONS:

The next time you feel your blood pressure rise as the result of an emotion, try using this Anger Management Chatterbox—a.k.a., paper fortune teller, cootie catcher, salt cellar, whirlybird—to get you back on track. When I did this workbook with my mother, she said that even though she's retired, she doesn't have time for crafts. Actually she said, "**Who has time for crafts?!**" In hindsight, maybe I shouldn't have told her not to hold anything back...

If you also have no time for crafts, you can substitute the cheat sheet in the back of the book—and thank my Mom—instead.

(cheat sheet can be found on p. 111)

Anger Management Chatterbox

To do this activity, start by cutting out the square.

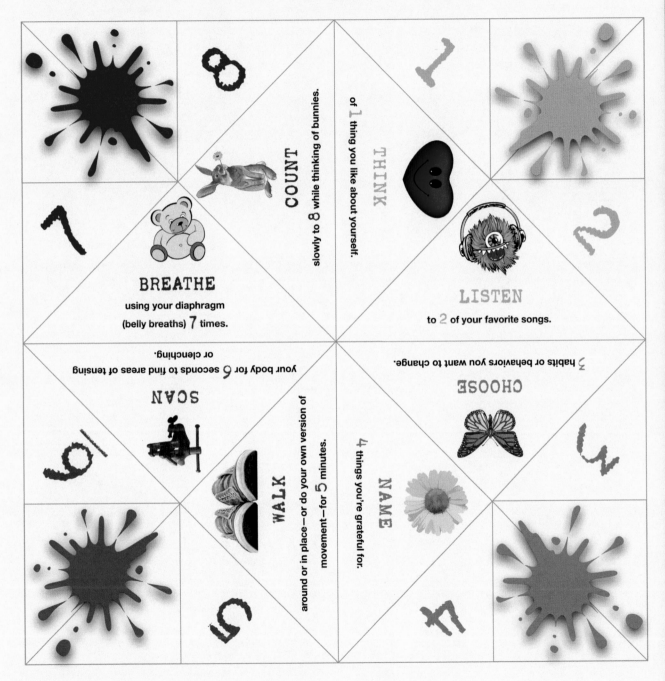

COUNT
slowly to 8 while thinking of bunnies.

THINK
of 1 thing you like about yourself.

BREATHE
using your diaphragm
(belly breaths) 7 times.

LISTEN
to 2 of your favorite songs.

SCAN
your body for 6 seconds to find areas of tensing
or clenching.

CHOOSE
3 habits or behaviors you want to change.

WALK
around or in place—or do your own version of
movement—for 5 minutes.

NAME
4 things you're grateful for.

Turn to p. 37 for instructions on how to fold this.

STEP 1

Once you've cut out the square, flip it so you don't see the images. To make creases, **fold and unfold** the square evenly along the diagonal, once in each direction.

STEP 2

Fold each of the four color corners to the center so that when you're done, all four colors form a diamond.

STEP 3

You should now have a smaller square that looks like the one above.

STEP 4

Flip the square over so you see the descriptions and images.

STEP 5

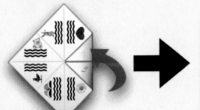

Fold each of the four numbered corners to the center so that when you're done, the colors are on the opposite side.

STEP 6

You should now have a smaller square that looks like the one above.

STEP 7

Fold that in half, keeping the colors on the outside.

STEP 8

Pull the color flaps out slightly to make space for your fingers beneath them. Then fold the right and left points inward till they touch.

STEP 9

One person picks a color. Open that flap so you see four numbers.

STEP 10

The same person picks one of those numbers and opens that flap to reveal the proposed anger reduction method.

Chapter 9 » What My Search Results Say About Me

OBJECTIVE

Enlarge your search IQ so you can be a more conscious consumer of Internet search engine results.

REMEMBER

Search algorithms may be programmed by people, but they operate without emotion. You, on the other hand, do not.

Filter bubble, a term coined by Eli Pariser, landed among my list of most-overused terms after the 2016 presidential election. That could be because I—like nearly everyone else—was in my own. If you're not familiar with the idea, it means that because of *personalized* searches and website algorithms, many of us live relatively unexposed to points of view that don't actively support our own, meaning our own *beliefs* are essentially repeated back to us and thereby reinforced.

This is similar to but not the same as an echo chamber. In music, an echo chamber is nothing more than an enclosed space used to produce sound reverberation; in political and philosophical terms, that enclosed space forms from the undermining and ridiculing of viewpoints that differ from your own. Unlike with musical reverb, however, the absorption of sound in a political echo chamber seems only to amplify its effect.

If you're good with that or if you don't believe it actually impacts your thoughts, I'm not here to convince you otherwise. I can't say with certainty that it does. The goal is just to challenge biases that can emerge when what we already know gets amplified and when sources of conflicting information get labeled "untrustworthy" merely because they lie outside our bubble.

I'm reminded of an apt parable most often attributed to the Cherokee: A grandfather talks about battling two wolves—conflicting impulses—inside himself. When asked which one wins, he thoughtfully replies "The one I feed."

This applies not only to impulses but to emotions as well. So the next time you go from zero to sixty, or from *sage* to *rage*, take care which one you feed, before the wrong one opens its mouth.

ACTIVITY INSTRUCTIONS:

Popular search engines so dominate the way we gather information that their names have become action verbs. While I don't have the slightest idea how algorithms for Google or Bing or any other search engine work, I can say with certainty that personalized search results more or less ensure you're going to see a list of sites and ads related to topics you've already searched (or possibly just talked about in front of any device with an active microphone). In other words, ideas that feel more or less in line with what you believe.

So rather than making any claims that could turn obsolete the next minute a major search engine tweaks its algorithm, let's do a comparison. Select one of your hot-button issues. Type it into a search engine on your most-used device, and see what comes up. Have the other person search it on their most-used device. Compare your first page of results. Then do the same with one of the other person's hot-button issues.

When you're done, search the reverb pedal below and see if it *resonates* with you as a way to get outside your bias zone and access resources geared toward accuracy and non-partisan advocacy.

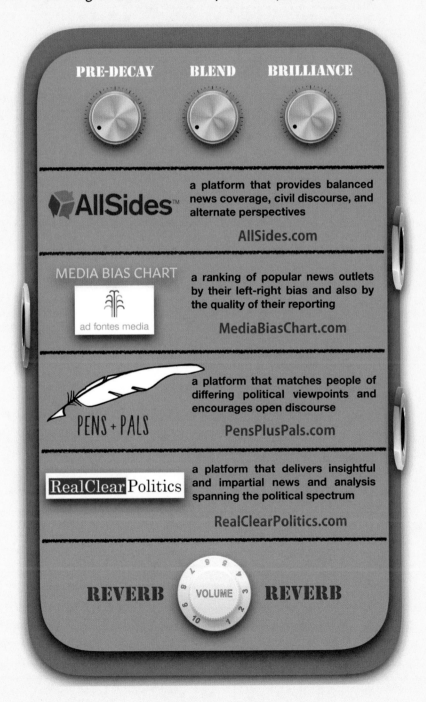

Chapter 10 » One Person's Junk Mail is Another Person's Treasure

OBJECTIVE

Help you rethink your relationship to political emails.

REMEMBER

Your political junk mail is someone else's news.

I get a lot of email, a good chunk of it as a prime target for marketers. To help deal with this apparent fact of our modern lives, email providers use a spam filter, which does something along the lines of relocating whatever they consider unwanted email into a folder marked—for the most part appropriately—Junk.

Sure, occasionally the filter weeds out an email I actually need—ironically, usually ones I send to myself—but for the most part, spam just gives me another reason to question how many hours or months or quite possibly *years* of my life I've spent deleting email. Seriously, think about how often you press the delete key. It adds up.

If you're politically active, chances are good you'll get targeted not only by your own chosen political party but by the opposing party as well. Little known fact: there is technically no such thing as political spam. Political messages are protected under the First Amendment and as such, are not required to abide by the same laws as commercial bulk email, which doesn't stop many of them from being delete-worthy.

Also, a forwarded political email rarely changes anyone's mind, so if you're tempted to share a political email with someone who disagrees with you, please think about the reason you're doing it and see if it in any way coincides with the outcome you'd like to happen. At the very least, fact-check it on Snopes.com or a similar website before you hit send. Then take a deep breath and go on with your day.

IF YOU NEED A LAUGH:

You may wonder why the junk that clutters our inboxes is even called spam. Etymologists seem to agree that it originates with the 1970 Monty Python's Flying Circus SPAM® skit. Search for it online and watch it with the other person, if possible. It's under five minutes, and though I'm in no way endorsing piracy—or Vikings, for that matter—you can find it on YouTube. Watching it should tell you all you need to know about why the term means junk mail.

ACTIVITY INSTRUCTIONS:

Find one piece of political junk email that you disagree with. Don't click on anything in it, and definitely don't download it because junk mail may contain viruses meant to harm your device. Just run a mental highlighter over anything you think the other person would agree with. Then read it to the other person. Do NOT forward it.

Since you're learning to ask how the other person sees an issue, go ahead and ask. If you were wrong about anything you thought the other person would agree with, admit it and apologize. Even if you were right about this particular issue, asking questions will help you use this sort of curiosity or inquisitiveness as your default.

When you're done, delete the email and go get a drink of water. Because staying hydrated affects your mood, your memory, your motor skills, and your ability to stay civil when you disagree.

For serious cases of spam or phishing, use the following to find out how to report the offending email.

REPORTING SPAM

The **CAN-SPAM Act (2003)** is a U.S. law that sets national standards for the dissemination of commercial email as enforced by the Federal Trade Commission. This doesn't include political emails—they are protected under the First Amendment—but you can report spam and scams to the organizations below.

Federal Trade Commission

You can report spam as well as scams, identity theft, and more to the FTC Complaint Assistant. They don't resolve your complaint but might use it to investigate or prosecute a crime: www.ftccomplaintassistant.gov.

FDA Office of Regulatory Affairs

The U.S. Food and Drug Administration's Office of Regulatory Affairs (ORA) accepts reports of emails that involve potentially fraudulent claims about medical devices or products. Report via email: webcomplaints@ora.fda.gov.

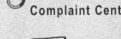

Internet Crime Complaint Center

Use the FBI's Internet Crime Complaint Center (IC3) to report cyber crimes including Internet fraud. The FBI analyzes the information and notifies the appropriate federal, state, local, and/or international agencies: www.ic3.gov.

Email Providers

Most email providers include a method for marking email as spam, but you can also report the offending email to them directly. Use a search engine to find out how: "[my email provider] report spam."

Banking Institutions

Banking institutions want you to report phishing attempts to them. Use a search engine to find out how: "[my banking institution] report spam" or call them directly. If you've been the victim of an Internet financial crime, report it to the IC3 above.

NOTES

Part Four: Debates

Chapter 11 » Finding Common Ground During an Earthquake

OBJECTIVE

Create a collaborative climate by understanding what causes seismic upheaval in yourself and the other person during a heated disagreement.

REMEMBER

To consider how your strained relationship has affected not just you but the other person, too.

Seeking common ground, especially during turbulent times, can often make you feel like the lone seal in an ocean of sharks, but this sort of vulnerability is required.

What most problem-solvers understand is that one-sided victories leave a lot of stirred-up emotions in their wake. You might reach your immediate goal, but it also creates resentments or flat-out enemies. This is not what we're trying to achieve here.

So before we dive deeper, ask yourself:

🔸 *What do you want your relationship with the other person to look like moving forward?*

_____
_____

🔸 *What are your options if the quality of your conversations doesn't improve?*

_____
_____

🔸 *What will it cost you and the other people in your life if you're unable to find a way to talk productively with that person?*

_____
_____

The reason finding common ground with an opponent can feel earth-shattering isn't only because of outer turmoil. Underneath anyone's exterior beliefs and motivations lie core issues that can put a person in a defensive, hostile, and antagonistic frame of mind. This helps conflicts stay unresolved and festering.

You need to become aware of these interior earthquakes, the agitated fissures that—if they remain hidden—will break down any real shot at productive conversation and a healthier understanding of yourself and the other person.

And in case you were worried about the seal, you can both use flexible thinking to maneuver out of this vulnerable position unscathed.

ACTIVITY INSTRUCTIONS:

To see what kind of shaky ground we carry around with us inside, write down your top 3 *personal concerns* in life. Not the stuff that government officials make policy on, but all that other stuff that makes us wonder what we're doing here on this rotating rock.

1. _____

2. _____

3. _____

What do you think are the other person's top 3 personal concerns?

1. _____

2. _____

3. _____

Finally, what are the other person's actual top 3 personal concerns?

1. _____

2. _____

3. _____

If you're having a hard time coming up with life concerns, have a look at the emotions inside this FEAR word salad. What worries accompany these words?

If your ideas about the other person's concerns differ from reality, what might this say about your own fears or concerns, both for yourself and for the other person?

Chapter 12 » Hands Off!

Identify the needs and values that stand behind certain absolutes in our lives.

REMEMBER

If something brings up intense emotion, it's usually related to a deep need we have. This is as true for us as it is for the other person.

We all have it: something in life that is yours alone. If you can't *identify* it for yourself, people who share your life can generally help you out. It might be a *favorite* mug, your journal, vintage Star Wars memorabilia, an autographed baseball, or your car, motorcycle, or truck. Whatever it is, chances are good that others understand the no-touch policy, and chances are even better that you helped them in some way to understand it.

We tend to have hands-off boundaries for a variety of reasons. If it's a favorite mug, your biggest concern might be breakage, but what else? Underneath our most guarded values and possessions lie the undeniable human needs and motivations common to us all.

To help understand root causes, a Japanese inventor named Sakichi Toyoda came up with a method to get to the bottom of manufacturing issues: asking "why" five times to locate the source of the problem.

Once you learn to recognize underlying causes in yourself, you may become more curious about investigating them in others and appreciating their fears and concerns as you do your own. *Why?* Because kindness towards others makes you happier. *Why?* Because the more you do it, the better you'll feel. *Why?* Because compassion, like cruelty, is contagious. *Why?* Well, what kind of person do you want to be? And *why?*

ACTIVITY INSTRUCTIONS:

Have a good look at your hands-off item. If you have more than one, choose whichever upsets you most at the thought of someone damaging it. If you can't put the item in front of you, substitute a photo or some other representation of it. You can write it down instead, but seeing it usually brings up more relatable emotions.

What does this item represent to you? Use the *5 Whys* method to uncover the needs behind your hands-off policy.

For example, if your hands-off item is a coffee mug and you don't want it to break, you might ask: *Why* would that bother me? Maybe your answer is: *I can't replace it. Why* can't I replace it?

Because a deceased relative gave it to me. Why did she give it to me? Because she knew I would value it. Why would she think that? Because I'm someone who values family. Why do I value family? Because it reminds me that people will cherish me after I'm gone. Because it helps me know that I am loved. Because it makes me feel safe. Why?

You get the point. You don't need to stop at 5 "whys." Keep digging until you land on something that feels like a revelation. To make this more interactive, have the other person ask you *Why?* That way, s/he gets used to questioning in a curious, non-judgmental way, and you get used to having your ideas challenged in that same curious, non-judgmental way. Then reverse.

When you're done, if the 5 Whys haven't already answered this, ask for the story of exactly how the hands-off item was acquired, the history behind the object itself (especially if it was handmade), and how it got transported over the years to keep it safe, as well as any story about the giver, if appropriate.

While listening, see if you can identify any deep-seated needs related to the item that can help you understand the other person's reality. Even if that doesn't work, get in the habit of asking *Why?* Then listen to responses in ways that give you new information rather than simply lighting up when something confirms what you already know.

If you get to a point at which you've exhausted your answers but none seems revelatory or meaningful, try accessing your emotions by tacking this onto the end of your last answer: *Because it makes me feel _____.*

My biggest concern about my hands-off item is _____.
"Why does this worry me?"

Put your answer here:

Why? →

Why? →

Why? ↓

Why? ←

Why? ←

For a bigger challenge, use the 5 Whys with one of your hot-button issues. Break it down in the same way, and see if you find any similar values to those of your hands-off item. Even if you're not ready to share this part with the other person, use it as a way to understand why the issue evokes such strong responses in you.

Chapter 13 » Sorting Out the Issues

OBJECTIVE

Discover which issues truly matter to you and consider some reasons why they do.

REMEMBER

Our hot-button issues are rooted in our different experiences and how we interpret them. That is why what matters to you might not matter to me and vice versa.

We sort everything from email to laundry, beans to buttons, flower pots, screws, and even *houses* in a school called Hogwarts. Sorting give us structure and routine, which some people *love*, others tolerate, and some just flat out avoid. You know who you are.

Or do you?

The first step in solving any problem usually means some recognition of where it fits with our core selves. When we try to solve problems or come up against someone who disagrees with us, it offers the chance to clarify why we believe what we do.

Our ability to do this has a lot to do with our individual tolerance for dissent. But even if your tolerance is not particularly high at the moment, it will gradually increase when you take incremental steps toward your growth edges. Before doing that, however, we need to sort out which issues truly matter to us.

ACTIVITY INSTRUCTIONS:

So many issues, so little time. Have a look at the items on pp. 50-51 and notice how you feel. Choose 3 issues for each of the following categories:

HOT: These could get you into hot water. Highly emotional. Topics that blast you from zero to rage in under three seconds.

WARM: These bother you but not enough to scald your tongue talking about them. You have an opinion but understand why some people disagree with your point of view.

COLD: These rank low on issues you care about. You can talk about them without needing a reminder to keep an open mind. They're important to someone, but you have other things on your grey matter.

We're going to put these issues through the wringer and break them down for better understanding. You'll use them in the worksheets that follow.

1. _____

2. _____

3. _____

1. _____

2. _____

3. _____

1. _____

2. _____

3. _____

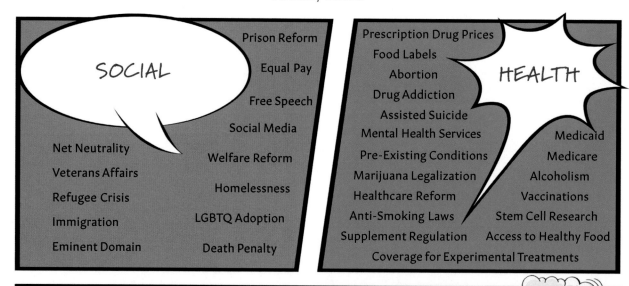

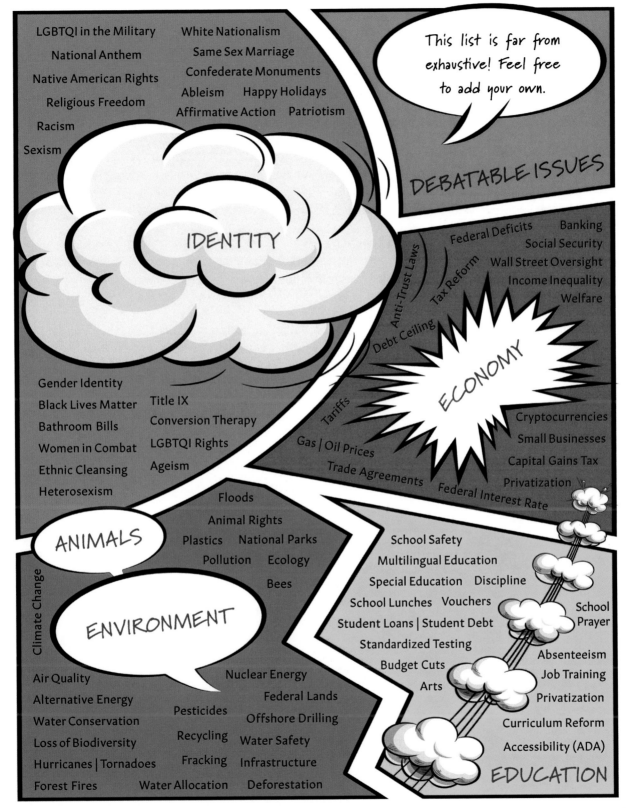

More on Sorting Out the Issues

So now you can list some of your HOT, WARM, and COLD issues. So what, right? It's not like you didn't know what you and the other person disagreed about before you saw it in writing.

The problem isn't that we don't know what bothers us. We just don't know what to do about it.

Most of us talk around or over or through people who disagree with us because we've never stopped to consider the fundamental beliefs behind our own points of view. People will always have distinct experiences and attach even more distinct meanings to them, but in order to have reasonable conversation about our disagreements, *how* we disagree not *what* we disagree about needs to change.

Ideologies basically break down into beliefs about how the world around us works or should work. Any ideology usually resonates most when it benefits us in some way, which should be our first clue that bias plays a part in shaping our beliefs. Way too often, we identify biases in others without looking at our own, mostly because we assume ours are correct and everyone else's are idiotic.

The extended part of this activity is meant to provide a better understanding about the belief system behind some of your issues: how that system gets reinforced, whether you've ever considered alternatives, and what sorts of real-world examples you base your particular beliefs on.

There is no judgment. You're just trying to learn something about yourself and about the other person. Judging—including jumping to conclusions, pigeonholing, and labeling—gets in the way of learning.

This is a judgment-free zone.

EXTRA ACTIVITY INSTRUCTIONS:

This activity gives you the chance to *dig* *deeper* into your HOT, WARM, and COLD issues. When you're done, share your answers with the other person. Just make sure to use the skills you've learned for *productive* conversation and start with the least antagonistic issue first.

Select 1 of your *COLD* issues: _____

Select 1 of your WARM issues: _____

Select 1 of your HOT issues: _____

Use your selected *COLD* issue and answer the following questions about it:

1. Why do you think this issue doesn't irk you as much as your *HOT* issues?

   _____

2. Write down one real-world example that contradicts your belief (e.g., You believe space exploration is a waste of resources, but what if a space mission discovered a cure for cancer on Mars?).

   _____

3. Could a contradiction make you reconsider your belief? If yes, how? If not, why not?

   _____

Use your selected *WARM* issue and answer the following questions about it:

1. What is one merit about the current policies regarding this issue? In other words, one thing you like about the situation as is, whether the current administration is responsible for it or not.

   _____

2. List at least two real-world examples upon which you've based your ideas about this issue?

   _____

3. Have you figured out how to fold fitted sheets? What do you think this indicates about your personality?

   _____

Use your selected *HOT* issue and answer the following questions about it:

1. What positive reinforcement do you get for your belief about it? In other words, who or what evidence in the real world strengthens your belief about this issue?

   _____

2. Would you rethink your position on this issue if you no longer received positive reinforcement for it? If so, why? If not, why not?

   _____

3. Why might the source of positive reinforcement listed above have more power to affect your beliefs than anything the other person says or believes?

   _____

Chapter 14 » If You Can't Say Something Nice...

OBJECTIVE

Observe how our opinions can be formed by assumptions that don't reflect reality.

REMEMBER

We are all imperfect human beings. Too often, we apply that truth to others using a magnifier and to ourselves using the reverse end of a telescope.

We all know how the sentence ends: *If you can't say something nice, don't say anything at all.* But the reason behind keeping your mouth shut has very little to do with productive communication. It's polite but not honest—and for our purposes, we need both.

Maybe the saying should go: *If you can't say something nice, try changing your point of view.*

We all have assumptions about others that we believe are right but could turn out to be false or incomplete. And while assumptions are definitely an efficient way to process the world, believing that our own opinions are right and those who disagree are (*fill in the blank*) does nothing to promote productive conversation or even civil discord.

Our political opinions form out of self-interest, life experiences, and ideas about what constitutes the common good—assumptions we make about how to serve our very human needs. The choice to challenge these assumptions is yours.

When you approach difficult conversations, ask yourself what you hope to gain from the experience. If your answer is, "change the other person's mind" or "make the other person see my point of view," you'll probably wind up frustrated. Effective communication comes from listening and just as importantly, getting comfortable with nuance and complexity. There's no shortage of either in politics or problem-solving.

ACTIVITY INSTRUCTIONS:

You may have seen this sort of fold-in before, especially if you ever picked up *MAD Magazine.* Just fold the right arrow over the star so it meets with the left to reveal the hidden picture and answer to the question. You can cut out the page if it makes it easier. See whether you and the other person come up with the same conclusion.

(folded version can be found on p. 112)

WHAT CAN YOU SAFELY ASSUME ABOUT ASSUMPTIONS?

» FOLD PAGE OVER THE STAR SO THE ARROWS MEET »« ✸ FOLD PAGE OVER THE STAR SO THE ARROWS MEET »« «

» ✸ «

WHEN THREADBARE ARGUMENTS HEIGHTENED THE HOLLERING IN PREDICTABLY TENDENTIOUS WAYS, A HATE VETO STUNTED OBNOXIOUS GROUPTHINK.

NOTES

Part Five: News Cycles

Chapter 15 » My News is Better Than Your News

OBJECTIVE

Increase your ability
to tolerate other
points of view.

REMEMBER

When it comes to
discussing news, replays
and direct quotes are
your new best friends.

Given the public's amplified *hunger* for news at all hours, it's hard to believe that the first TV news shows lasted a mere 10 minutes. Those days are long gone. We live in a time when you don't have to seek out the *news*; you have to seek out ways to avoid it.

If you turn to news specifically for politics, chances are high that you have a favorite source; chances are even higher that it has what many consider an ideological bent. This means you're likely to watch news that more or less agrees with your point of view. This doesn't necessarily mean your news source has abandoned accurate reporting, just that the stories tend to get told from a perspective that favors a particular point of view.

Yet no matter how different its source, news fulfills at least one need we all share: wanting to feel like we have a road map to understanding our lives.

Whether we admit it or not, uncertainty is difficult and anxiety-inducing. We seek knowledge to feel like we have more control over our lives because in spite of what our inspirational coffee mug or the poster at work tells us, life is frequently random and unfair. (Give yourself points if your coffee mug or poster tells you life is frequently random and unfair.)

So for a change, don't skip the formality. Pretend the other person is someone you just met and try forming a connection based on mutual respect. Ease into your areas of contention. Real connections don't come by shouting the loudest or insisting you're right. They come by identifying the basic needs that lie behind what you're feeling and then taking a risk to share those needs with another.

Beyond food, water, & shelter, some needs that can cause anxiety are:

- sense of community
- security and safety
- career and job retention
- financial stability
- mind and body health

- creative pursuits
- control over life decisions
- life purpose and goals
- status and recognition
- intimacy and attention

So, the next time you're feeling angry about politics, ask yourself if your ability to satisfy any of these needs is threatened because of policies—actual or potential—on that issue. Instead of focusing on your anger, spend at least as much time asking: *What am I afraid of?* Your first answer isn't likely to produce any surprises, so make sure to follow up with: *Why am I afraid of that?*

Use what you've learned about the 5 *Whys* (see Chapter 12 if you need a reminder) to drill down to a fear related to your own well-being or the well-being of someone you love. If you get to this level of self-understanding, try sharing what you learned with the other person and see if you can turn a grudge match into something productive: an opportunity for connection.

This doesn't require you to change your views or even pretend you're not upset. You just have to respect the fact that you're talking to another human being who underneath it all has fears and anxieties, too.

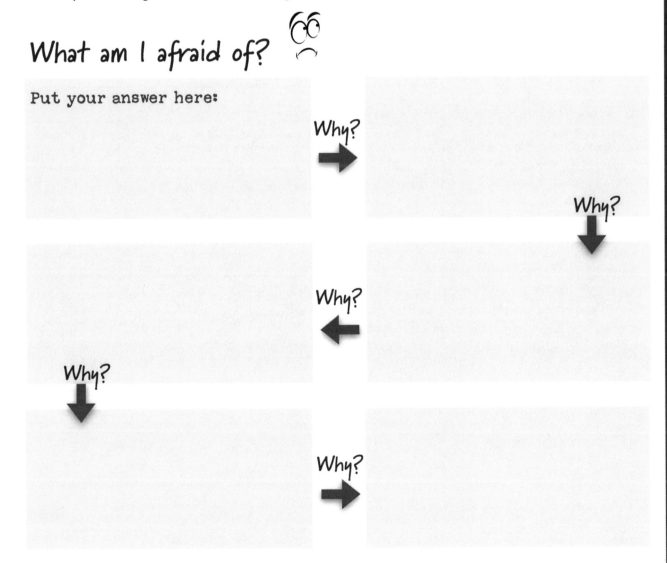

ACTIVITY INSTRUCTIONS:

You might find the next part eye-opening—or vomit-inducing—but we're all in this together, so hang on.

Be honest: Do you research a story further after you've seen or heard about it from your chosen news? I don't mean tuning to a similar show that merely regurgitates the information. I mean, do you seek out an alternate, ideally non-partisan news source? Do you see what another side of the issue looks like?

If, like most of us, your answer is a larger-than-life *no*, it might be time to do something about that.

In order to understand why people believe as they do, it's important to know what they use to make their decisions. Granted, not all of it comes from news sources, but if knowledge is a chain of accumulated information, it's only as strong as its least truthful link.

For this activity, you need to know the other person's preferred show for getting political news. Don't presume you know it, even if you can hear it in the background during your conversations.

My preferred news source: _____

Other person's preferred news source: _____

Just thinking about the other person's news may feel like an unwanted jolt, but in the interest of learning to tolerate points of view that differ from your own, for one day, watch—or listen to—the other person's news source as *well as* your own. You don't have to tune in for the whole day. Thirty minutes to an hour should do. Just make sure you and the other person are both tuned in to the same show on the same day.

If each of your preferred shows is on at the same time and you don't have access to a replay or recording, just split the shows between two nights. Now comes the hard part. OK, the harder part. You cannot consume news from any other source for the entire day, meaning you'll need to stay off social media. I highly recommend unplugging from social media at least once weekly anyway—your neurons have better things to do. Oh, and if your usual commute or workday includes talk radio or news-related podcasts (and they're not your or the other person's preferred news source), those get turned off, too.

Finally, try not screaming at the TV during this activity. You are not tuning in for a debate, just to get information.

If at all possible, record the shows, even if you're watching live. You're going to want those direct quotes when you're trying to discuss it with the other person.

SHOWS TO WATCH	DATE	TIME
_____	_____	_____
_____	_____	_____

When thinking about what you liked and didn't like, be specific. What topics do you think they paid too much or too little attention to? How does the tone of voice impact you?

My news source (main topics/stories discussed):

_____ _____ _____

What I liked: _____

What I disliked (can't be nothing): _____

Other person's news source (main topics/stories discussed):

_____ _____ _____

What I liked (can't be nothing): _____

What I disliked: _____

Next, write down the name of at least one reporter or host from the other person's news outlet with whom you'd share a meal.

_____

What question would you ask if you knew that person had to answer honestly? Get creative. Think of what might reveal the humanity of that individual rather than just reflexively asking a question you think you know the answer to. For example, my mother wanted to ask a news commentator: _What's your favorite charity and how do you support it? Do you volunteer? If so, for what?_ While these questions would reveal something about the person who answered, they also tell me something about my Mom and what matters to her.

_____

Ask the same questions of the other person you're doing this workbook with. If your question doesn't apply, try adjusting it so they will. Hold any comments until the other person has finished speaking. In fact, you're under no obligation to come up with a response. Rather than trying to figure out what you're going to say or when to interject, stay accountable to the moment and continue cultivating your active listening skills.

Chapter 16 » What the Heck is a Policy Wonk?

OBJECTIVE

Have some fun discovering what you know, and consider that we often don't know as much as we think we do.

REMEMBER

Until the 1960s, most American high school students had three distinct courses in civics and government. Currently, only around 25% of Americans can name all three branches of our government.

The phrase itself—policy wonk—brings to mind that strange creature who likes the technical details of government and who studies and develops political strategies and *principles*. Now, I like numbers as much as—maybe a little more than—the next *person*, but I have zero interest in walking neck-deep through the morass of our government's intricacies.

I'm not alone. Most of us don't get an adrenaline rush from policy, but don't let that scare you off. We can all learn more, and thankfully, being a good citizen doesn't require us to know every politically nuanced in-and-out. It may bring little joy to admit, but we need the wonks. And they need us. Without citizens, the government has nothing to do.

Although we offload a lot of civic responsibility to our government officials, good citizenship does require us to know *something*. Of course, politicians and citizens alike could stand to remember that we don't know what we don't know, which is OK. It's thinking we know everything that often brings emotional rushes to judgment with little basis in fact.

So start small, but start. A good citizen is always a work in progress.

ACTIVITY INSTRUCTIONS:

This activity is designed to familiarize you with some of the questions from the civics portion of the U.S. naturalization test (part of the requirement for citizens of another country to become citizens of the U.S.) by using a simple board game (pp. 64-65); granted, minus a cardboard box and the pieces that would make up a typical board game. I not-so-secretly hope you and the other person will have fun figuring out how to get the most out of this, even if you're not in the same room with each other.

I understand that immigration causes a lot of tempers to flare. If you plan to discuss it with the other person, try to remember that immigration has many facets. We're not trying to agree on every detail, just have reasonable debate.

Talk about what you hope immigration policies can accomplish and remember that civility and citizenship have the same *root*.

Getting Set Up

1. Use a standard die OR the ace (1) through 6 cards of any suit in a deck of cards OR write 1-6 on six pieces of scrap paper and fold them. Whichever option you use, the numbers should go from 1 to 6.

2. Find something to use as game pieces* or cut out the circles on the question and answer sheets (pp. 113-114).

How to Play

Everyone rolls the die (or picks a card or a folded piece of paper with a number on it). The person with the highest number goes first, and play continues left (clockwise). Even if you're not in the same room, I'm sure you can figure it out!

Each square on the game board has a number in one of its corners. Everyone starts before square #1. You'll notice that there are steps and slides. Unlike in similar games, landing on one of these doesn't mean you automatically follow that path. Read on.

ON YOUR TURN
Start at the ✶. If you roll (or pick) a 4, for instance, your game piece will wind up on square #4. It's OK for two or more game pieces to be on a square at the same time. Continue play until someone reaches square #96. You must land on it exactly. If your number would take you beyond square #96, wait until your next turn and try again. Unless you don't feel like playing that way. Then do whatever suits you.

GOING UP A STEP
If you land on square #17, #28, #35, #49, or #66, you'll have the opportunity to answer a question. Answer correctly, and you'll climb the ladder to the corresponding square above it. Answer incorrectly, and you'll stay on that square. Either way, play moves to your left.

GOING DOWN A SLIDE
If you land on square #21, #40, #53, #82, or #92, you'll have the opportunity to answer a question. Answer correctly, and you can stay where you are. Answer incorrectly, and you'll slide down to the square in the indicated row beneath it. Either way, play moves to your left.

Where are the Questions?!

The game questions (and answers) are on pp. 113-114 so you can tear them out or make a copy of them before you start playing. Flipping back and forth would send game pieces flying. Speaking of, some possible *game pieces are:

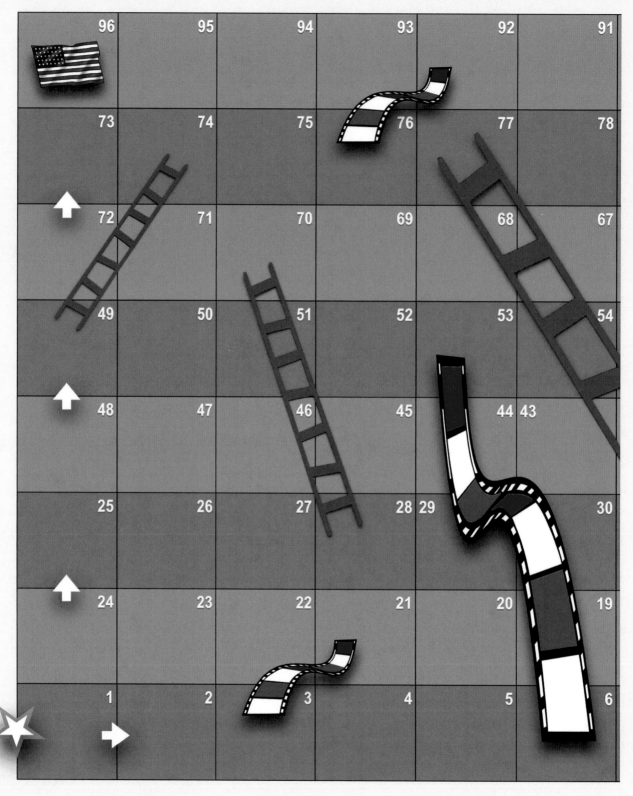

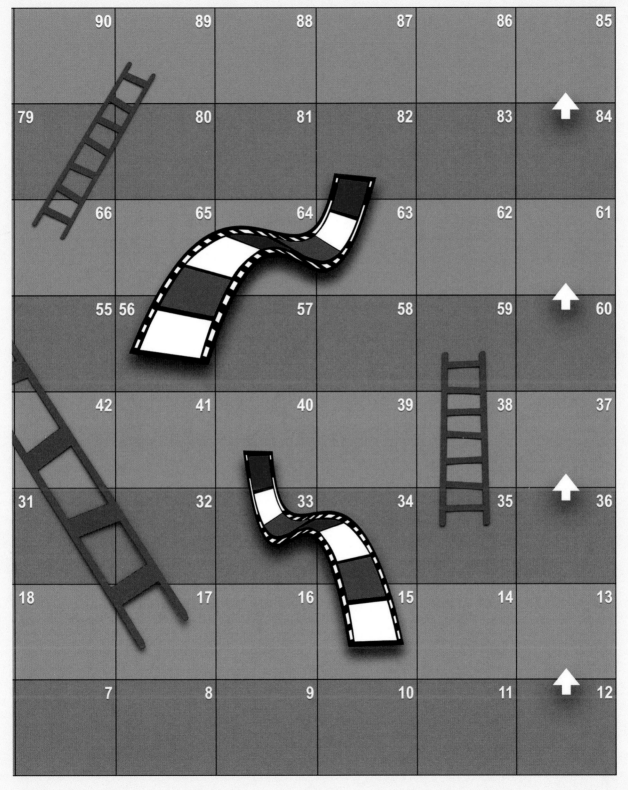

Chapter 17 » Should I Meditate or Call You?

OBJECTIVE

Help you decide whether to share political news with the other person.

REMEMBER

Sharing is not always caring.

Sharing. It sounds like a stellar idea or at the very least, an innocuous one. We share all kinds of things these days: cars, clothes, couches, songs, scooters, files, books, bikes, quotes, our location at any given time, and so much more. At this point, a whole *generation* has entered adulthood believing that *sharing* is a business model. That's not necessarily a bad thing.

Yet when it comes to the flow of ideas, we tend to let ourselves get a little too comfortable with generosity. Not only online but IRL (In Real Life), too.

The flow of ideas may be how we learn, but when it comes to politics, this flow can break relationships as often as it makes them. The not-so-new agitator in this equation? Emotions.

But not just any emotions. Primarily those that cause a spike in our adrenaline, like anger and anxiety, joy and awe.

Coincidentally, this sort of arousal gets spread via our sympathetic nervous system, so sharing is almost in the definition. Ironically, however, the sympathetic nervous system is also a branch of the autonomic nervous system, which functions autonomously.

Are you confused? Bored? Annoyed? Don't worry. I'm using the above as an example of oversharing and how easily we can confuse our own emotional state (e.g., my personal excitement about word play and learning a new fact about the body) with information that may be of value to the receiver.

This also applies to political sharing. You hear a news story and think, *A-ha! This will change Pat's mind. I'll give Pat a call.* But it's not always that straightforward. Sometimes it's more like, *A-ha! This will be good for Pat to hear. It may even change Pat's mind. What should I have for dinner? I had pasta for lunch, so no more carbs. What was that chicken recipe that Pat gave me?*

The next thing you know you're talking to Pat, asking for the chicken recipe. It happens to be called Stars-and-Stripes Chicken, which reminds you about that news story, so you decide to share. Surprise! It doesn't change Pat's mind at all, but now Pat is mad at you, which makes you mad enough not to use the recipe, and you still don't know what you're having for dinner.

ACTIVITY INSTRUCTIONS:

Heightened arousal meets its match in meditation. The next time you hear a news story or a political tidbit you're tempted to share with the other person, have a look at the *Ten Stages* circle below and when you find your level of anger, match it with a reason to meditate.

If you don't feel like any part of the wheel applies or you just can't stand the thought of meditating, go through the flowchart on the following page before you call. You may have a different idea by the time you reach the end.

67

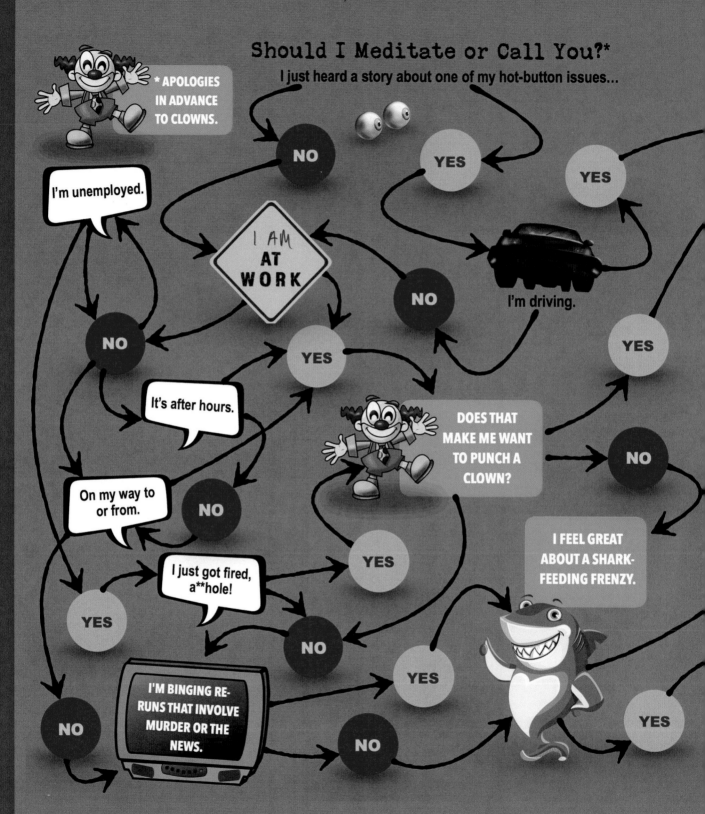